To Leiya,
Find magic in reading
as you travel to Peru with
Annabelle. Jan O'Neill
2005 ♡

Annabelle Alpaca
Travels to Peru

Written by Jan O'Neill
Illustrated by B.E. Anderson

Dedicated to my family for their continual support especially my parents,
Ray and Lorraine, and my sister, Barbara.
My deepest gratitude goes to my editor, Abbie.

-J.O.

A special Thank You to MeMe and Sam.

-B.A.

Annabelle awoke as the first ray of sunshine peeked through the barn and landed in her eyes. A cool, fall, Michigan breeze ruffled her locks and she shivered as she stood up. She stepped outside and joined Molly, the Angora goat, who was warming herself in the early morning sunshine.

"Good morning Molly," said Annabelle.

"Gee Annabelle, it is cold this morning," said Molly.

"Yes Molly, it is a little chilly, but it feels just like mornings did back home where I came from." As the two huddled together next to the barn, off in the distance the young alpaca crias (baby alpacas) and goat kids began a game of follow the leader.

"Annabelle?" asked Molly, "where did you come from?"

"Well Molly, alpacas come from South America. Some are from Bolivia or Chile but I came from Peru," said Annabelle.

"'Peru'? Where is that?" asked Molly.

Just then the crias and kid goats quit their game to get a drink of water. After they drank, they settled down to rest and Annabelle continued.

"Peru is a country that is very far from here. It is where I was born. My grandmother and grandfather still live there," said Annabelle.

"What was it like to live in Peru?" asked Marshmallow Fluff, a young Huacaya alpaca.

"Well, I was just a cria like you when I lived there, but I remember the mountains and the beautiful blue lakes," hummed Annabelle in thought. "I miss my grandmother and grandfather; I haven't seen them in four years." She whispered, "I wonder....hmmmm."

Just then, Banner, the Arabian horse, came trotting over. "Annabelle, why don't you go to Peru and visit your grandparents?" he suggested.

"Yes, Annabelle," said Molly, "you should go to Peru! Why don't you ask the farmer and his wife to take you there?"

"That is a good idea," said Annabelle. "I will ask them to take me back to Peru to visit my grandparents!"

"Can I go too?" asked Fluff. "I want to see Peru!"

"Sure, you can come along," said Annabelle as she walked toward the farmhouse, "if the farmer says he will take us."

♪"We're going to Peru, we're going to Peru," ♪ sang Fluff as she skipped through the barn. Tag, the gray barn cat, awoke to Fluff's song.

He lazily stretched his legs and asked, "Can I go to Peru with you, please Fluff, please?"

"I don't think so Tag, Peru is very far away and you are not used to long car rides," said Fluff.

One bright sunny morning, a couple of days later, the farmer's minivan backed up to the barn. Annabelle awoke early and was saying her last goodbyes to her barnyard friends when the farmer called for her. Molly ran up to the side of the van as Annabelle and Fluff hopped in.

"Oh Molly, I will miss everyone, but I think I will miss you most of all," hummed Annabelle. "Please watch over the crias and keep an eye on Tag and the chickens," she added.

"I will help her watch over the barn," neighed Banner, "don't worry Annabelle. Everything will be fine."

The barn yard friends waved and called goodbye as the van pulled away. The farmer's wife pulled out a map as they traveled down the highway.

"Look Annabelle and Fluff, this is where we are going," and she held up the map for the alpacas to see. "Here is where we are," and she pointed to Michigan on the map. "We will travel through these states," and she pointed to: Indiana, Illinois, Missouri, Arkansas, and Texas. "When we get here," and she pointed to the border of Texas, "we will enter Mexico."

"Then will we be in Peru?" asked Fluff.

"No Fluff," said the farmer's wife, "after we leave Mexico, we will travel through Central America which includes: Guatemala, Honduras, Nicaragua, Costa Rica, and Panama. Then we enter South America where we will travel by ferry around Columbia and continue through Ecuador." She pointed to it on the map.

"Then will we be in Peru?" pleaded Fluff.

"Yes Fluff, then we will finally be in Peru, Annabelle's homeland."

"It is a long, long, long way to Peru," hummed Fluff as she settled down for a nap.

They continued driving as the alpacas slept, and when they awoke the minivan was stopping at a picnic area next to Lake Michigan.

"Annabelle! Fluff!" called the farmer, "are you hungry?" The alpacas hopped out of the minivan and stretched their legs.

"Yes, I am a bit hungry," said Annabelle. The farmer's wife pulled the picnic basket out of the van and picked up the fluffy quilt stuffed with alpaca fiber (the soft, fluffy hair that is cut off alpacas once a year). As she unrolled the quilt onto the grass, out popped Tag the kitten.

"Oh Tag!" screamed the farmer's wife in surprise. "How did you get in that quilt?"

Annabelle and Fluff ran over and sniffed Tag. "Tag, is it really you?" asked Annabelle. The farmer came over to see what all the excitement was about.

"Oh Tag, you little stowaway! I guess you will be going to Peru with us," he said. Tag stood up and rubbed his body against the farmer's legs.

"Meow, I just wanted to be with Annabelle and Fluff," he said.

"Let's sit on the quilt and have our picnic," said the farmer's wife. "Tag, I did not pack anything for your lunch," she said, but I will share my sandwich with you."

The minivan rolled down the highway for days and days. Annabelle kept Fluff and Tag busy with quiet games of spotting interesting things out the window. When they became tired of the games, Annabelle would tell them stories until they fell asleep.

"Are we there yet?" Fluff asked. "I have to go potty," she cried." Shortly thereafter, the farmer pulled off the highway and stopped at a small building next to the Rio Grande River.

"You can go potty here Fluff," said the farmer's wife. As they all hopped out of the van, the farmer directed Annabelle, Tag, and Fluff to a grassy area in the trees. The farmer and his wife walked toward the building.

Back on the highway, the alpacas settled down for a long ride. The farmer's wife looked back and smiled at the kushed alpacas. The kushing position is when the alpacas lay on their stomach with their legs folded underneath them.

All of a sudden, Annabelle jumped up screaming, "Tag!!!! He is not here; we left him behind!" As the farmer turned the van around and they sped toward the rest area, Tag's head poked out of the quilt.

"Meow, here I am," he said. "Why are we going soooo fast?" he asked.

"Oh Tag, we thought we left you at the Rio Grande," explained the farmer's wife. "You really gave us a scare," she said, "but I am glad we didn't leave you alone at the rest area."

After a long week of travel, at last the minivan arrived in Peru. They stopped in a small village to buy some food and bottled water. The villagers were dressed in colorful clothes and had many unusual items displayed, including baskets filled with fruits and vegetables. Annabelle and Fluff walked along the road admiring the colorful woven blankets, knitted scarves, and beaded necklaces made by the ladies of the village. The farmer's wife purchased some potatoes, rice, water, and a couple of knitted hats. The farmer got directions to the farm where Annabelle's grandparents lived.

The next morning the minivan turned onto a dirt road. The van drove under an old faded sign that said "Rancho Rosa". In the distance, Annabelle could see black hills leading up to the snow crested peaks of the Andes Mountains. Fluff noticed the crisscross pattern of stones stacked on top of each other.

"Look at all of those stones, in row after row, how did they get like that?" asked Fluff.

"Well, the ranchers made fences with the stones to keep the alpacas in one area," replied the farmer.

"Alpacas!" cried Fluff. "I can see them over there!" They continued up the drive and were greeted by the ranchers and a friendly llama named Dudley.

Dudley took them to the pasture where Annabelle's grandparents were grazing. "Grandma! Grandpa!" Annabelle yelled in excitement. The older alpaca's eyes teared up as they saw Annabelle run toward them.

"Oh it's our little Annabelle," said Grandma. "You have grown so big since we saw you last." They hugged each other with their necks and sat under the shade of a large tree to visit. Annabelle began to think about the remainder of their vacation.

"Grandma and Grandpa, would you please join us as we visit some of the tourist attractions?"

"We would love to spend more time with you," said grandma.

"Yes, let's do it," said grandpa.

The next morning, Dudley watched as the minivan disappeared in a cloud of dust.

After a long day of travel the minivan came to a stop. "Where are we?" cried Fluff.

"This is Machu Picu," said the farmer.

"'Machu Picu', what is that?" asked Fluff.

"Tomorrow you will see what it is, we will rest for the night. In the morning we will board the train and travel high into the mountains," answered the farmer.

The next morning the train took them through the Sacred Valley of the Andes Mountains. At last the train came to a halt and they arrived at Machu Picu, also known as the ancient Peak. As Annabelle, Fluff, Grandma, Grandpa, and Tag stepped off the train, they were stunned by what they saw. The giant stone structures seemed to rise out of the middle of the jagged mountains.

"It's so beautiful," exclaimed Annabelle. The farmer and his wife, followed by the alpacas and the cat, toured the magnificent ruins for hours. Soon the train's whistle blew (choo, choo), and it was time to leave.

That night they slept under the stars.

"Today, we go to Chaccu, where we will help with a very special event that happens only once every three years. It's known as the 'vicuna round-up,'" said the farmer.

"What is a 'vicuna round-up'?" asked Fluff.

"Well a vicuna is a wild ancestor of the alpaca that roams freely in the Andes Mountains. Once every three years the local people round up the wild vicunas and shear their beautiful fiber, which is like giving them a hair cut. The villagers sell the fiber to help support their people," said the farmer's wife.

When they arrived at the Chaccu, the villagers had already herded the vicunas down from the mountains. The farmer and his wife helped the villagers move the herd of vicunas into the enclosure where they would stay until they were sheared. Annabelle, Fluff, Tag, and the older alpacas watched as the vicunas were sheared.

That night, the Chaccu ended with a festival of music and dancing.

The next morning the farmer called, "It's time to head home." On their way home, they dropped Grandma and Grandpa off at "Rancho Rosa" and they said their goodbyes.

"Please come to Michigan and visit us sometime," said Annabelle with a tear in her eye.

After a very, very long ride, the tired travelers arrived in Michigan.

"I can't wait to see Molly," said Annabelle. "I have missed her so much," she added. "I miss Banner, Ebony, and the crias," said Fluff.

Tag meowed, "I wonder if my catnip is still growing in the garden?"

When they arrived home, Annabelle called all of her barnyard friends. "I have a souvenir for all of you," she said. She set down a brightly colored woven bag and her friends took turns picking out hats, blankets, scarves, and beaded necklaces.

"I am so glad to be here! Peru is very nice but it's not home, <u>my home</u> is right here with all of you!" hummed Annabelle.

The End